# Everything Sleeps

Written by Emma Alagbary　　Illustrated by Hana Alagbary

Words Copyright © 2022 Emma Alaġbary
Illustrations Copyright © 2022 Hana Alaġbary

All rights reserved. This book or any portion thereof may not be reproduced or used in any manner without the express written permission of the copyright holder.

Published by Little Dragon Books

Dunedin, New Zealand

First Edition
Paperback

ISBN-13: 978-0-473-61776-9

littledragonbooks.com

# Everything Sleeps

Fish sleep with their eyes open.

Horses sleep standing up!

Bats sleep upside down.

Otters hold hands while they sleep.

Aww!

Giraffes take naps with their heads on their backs.

Dolphins sleep with one eye open.

Albatrosses take lots of tiny naps... while flying!

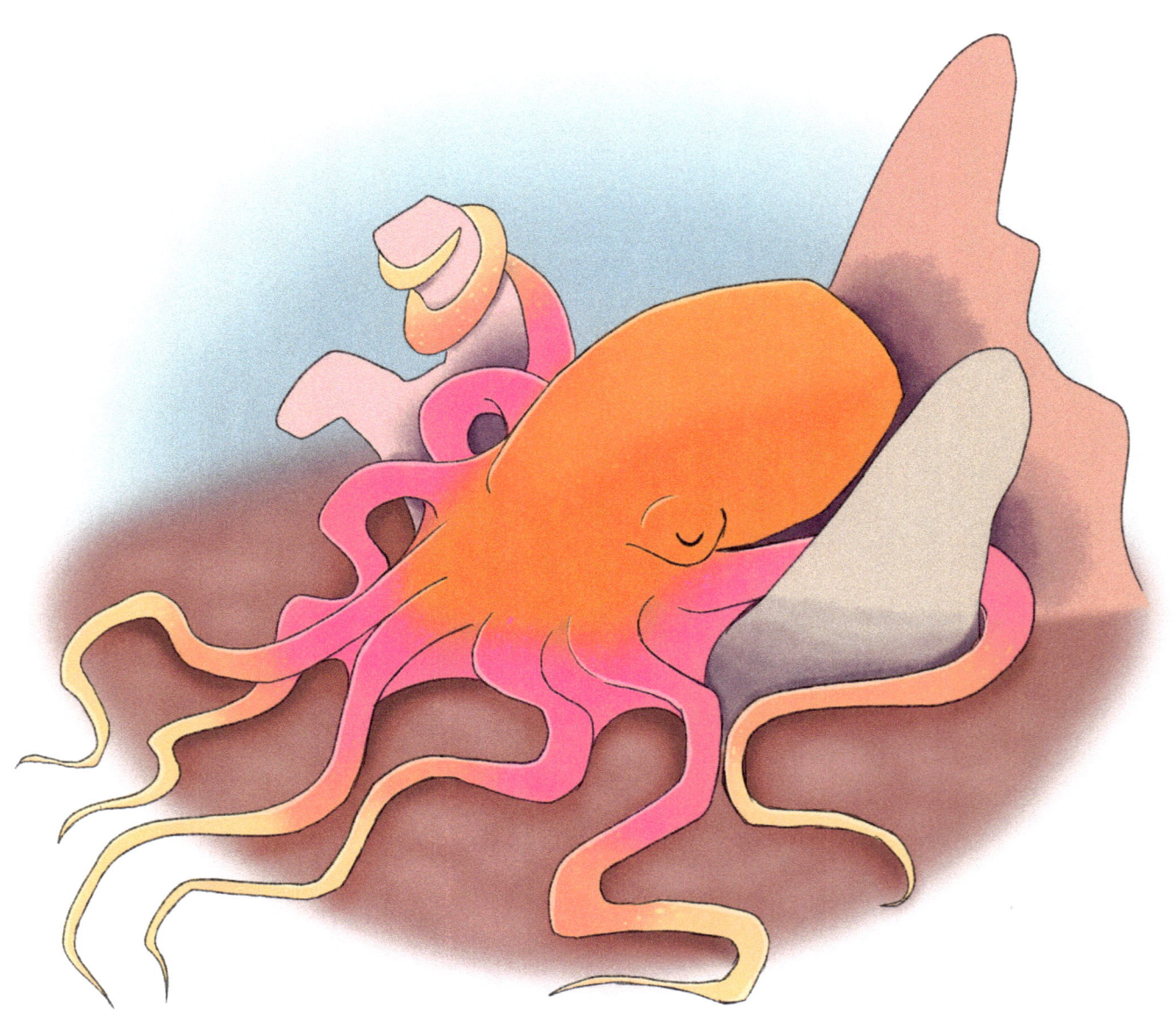

Octopi change color while they sleep.

Ducks sleep in rows.

Meerkats sleep in piles.

Sloths sleep for at least half the day.

Bears sleep all winter.

Snails sleep for years!

Gorillas sleep just like we do.

Babies sleep.

A lot!

Even grown-ups and big brothers and sisters sleep.

And you?
You sleep too, of course.

Good night!

# Different Ways To Sleep

Diurnal - Active during the day and asleep at night. Humans are diurnal.

Nocturnal - Active at night and asleep during the day. Animals like bats and hedgehogs are nocturnal.

Crepuscular - Most active during dawn and dusk and sometimes on cloudy days and bright nights. Animals like bears and cats are crepuscular.

Metaturnal or Cathemeral - Active at various times during the day and night. Lions and rabbits are metaturnal. Some animals that switch from diurnal to nocturnal with the seasons are considered metaturnal.

# Also Available in Bilingual
## Arabic-English and Māori-English Editions

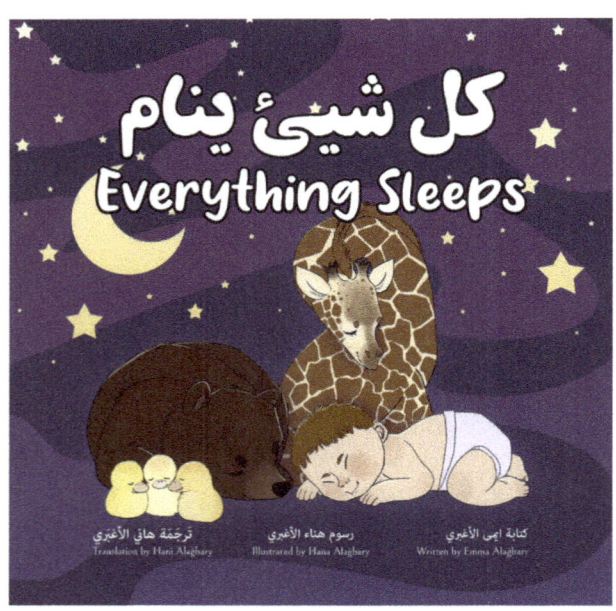
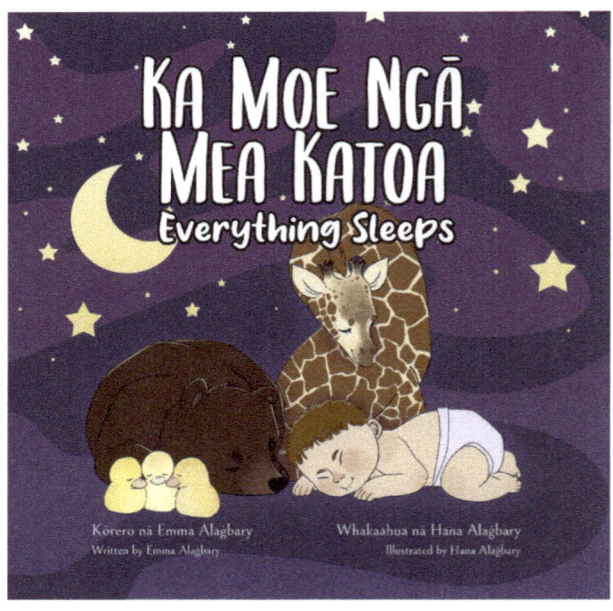

## Little Dragon Books
*treasures you can read*

Did your children enjoy this book?

We're an independent publisher, support us by:
Leaving a review on Amazon and Goodreads.
Signing up to our newsletter littledragonbooks.com/news.
Visiting our website and following our social media.
Asking your local library and bookstore to order our books.

littledragonbooks.com

## Meet the Author:
## Emma Alagbary

Emma is a lifelong artist and writer from New Zealand. She was born at the bottom of the South Island and grew up at the top of the North Island before moving to Chicago as a teenager. Emma has been a web and print designer for over 15 years and has worked in independent children's publishing for almost a decade.

## Meet the Illustrator:
## Hana Alagbary

Hana was born in Chicago and moved to New Zealand as a teenager. She is half Yemeni and half Kiwi, making her a true global citizen. Hana has been drawing and writing stories prolifically since she could hold a pen and made her debut as an independent illustrator at sixteen.

www.ingramcontent.com/pod-product-compliance
Lightning Source LLC
Chambersburg PA
CBHW061759290426
44109CB00030B/2899